VOICING
— THE —
SOUND
ETERNAL

TRANSFORMATIONAL POWER OF
SOUND AND CONSCIOUSNESS

MELISSA A. HIGGINBOTHAM

BALBOA.PRESS
A DIVISION OF HAY HOUSE

Balboa Press books may be ordered through booksellers or by contacting:

Balboa Press
A Division of Hay House
1663 Liberty Drive
Bloomington, IN 47403
www.balboapress.com
1 (877) 407-4847

Because of the dynamic nature of the Internet, any web addresses or
links contained in this book may have changed since publication and
may no longer be valid. The views expressed in this work are solely those
of the author and do not necessarily reflect the views of the publisher,
and the publisher hereby disclaims any responsibility for them.

The author of this book does not dispense medical advice or prescribe the use
of any technique as a form of treatment for physical, emotional, or medical
problems without the advice of a physician, either directly or indirectly. The
intent of the author is only to offer information of a general nature to help
you in your quest for emotional and spiritual well-being. In the event you use
any of the information in this book for yourself, which is your constitutional
right, the author and the publisher assume no responsibility for your actions.

Any people depicted in stock imagery provided by Getty Images are
models, and such images are being used for illustrative purposes only.
Certain stock imagery © Getty Images.

Print information available on the last page.

ISBN: 978-1-9822-4107-0 (sc)
ISBN: 978-1-9822-4109-4 (hc)
ISBN: 978-1-9822-4108-7 (e)

Library of Congress Control Number: 2020900439

Balboa Press rev. date: 02/18/2020

Contents

Foreword

Traditionally we were all taught that hope or hoping is placing ourselves in the future and therefore not manifesting what is needed in the present moment, the Now Point. Hope really means to expand within to encompass and allow all potentials of Source within self.

When we sing or tone from a consciousness space of Source, we start to expand within ourselves to allow all potentials of Source to ascend within and as the self. Thus the songs, the tones we sing, are actually sacred song. This is the gift we are giving ourselves and, through us, the potential for all others to realize it.

Introduction

If you want to find the secrets of the Universe, think in terms of energy, frequency, and vibration.

—Nikola Tesla

Do you ever really listen? Do you truly listen to the sounds of the earth around you? Or are the sounds of the earth masked by the sound of your thoughts and the endless noise of an intrusive, technologically driven daily routine?

We get up in the morning, and the first sound we hear is the alarm clock and then the drip-drip-drip of the coffee maker, the splash of the shower, and the morning news and weather on the television. Dashing out, we hear the slam of the door and then the roaring start of the car as we turn on the ignition. We hurriedly switch on the radio for traffic news and then join the endless stream of cars honking their horns and blaring music until we finally arrive at work.

There we hear the slap of soles against the floor and the whirr of small supply carts passing before we reach our offices and the phones ring, the computers boot up, and doors open and close as people arrive. Some come into work; others seek assistance. It's an endless parade of people and an infinite drone of constant noise that we learn to block out on some levels. But the toll is taken, and we end the day exhausted.

When the people leave, we sigh and think, *Oh, blessed silence.*

But is it silent? The people may be gone, but the computers are still humming, the air-conditioning is whirring, and the refrigerator, printer, fax machine, and phone all emit some level of noise. We have just learned to block it out, to compartmentalize it. But it is there in the background, a steady curtain of noise blocking out the sound of the earth around us, obstructing our ability to truly listen to all levels of creation.

The first step in sound healing is to listen—to listen and to understand. Do you know what it means to hear the sound behind the sound? Listening is much more than just hearing notes or melodies with your ears. True listening is aligned with cognition, a sense/feel type of knowing. Sometimes this sense/feel knowing is an awareness of sound itself as waves and consciousness.

Sound Healing and Consciousness

You are an orchestra of sound. As you learn to play each instrument of the orchestra within, you find that the journey always takes you back to consciousness, back to the beginning, back to God-Source. In the beginning was the Word, and the Word was sound.

All creation came out of sound, a standing wave vibration of sound, which became light as it moved out into manifestation. In this sense, we are light beings, but in reality, we are composed of both sound and light, and with the right vision, we can be seen and heard as standing wave pillars of sound-light. Because everyone is composed of and created by sound, sound affects the energetic crystalline structure underlying matter.

Experiments conducted by Hans Jenny, a Swiss physicist, showed that sound/vibration caused sand on top of a plate to form patterns. Different sounds formed distinct patterns. This implies that if sound could form patterns in the sand, it could also shape patterns within our atomic and energetic structures. It is interesting to theorize about the shape or patterns different instruments or singing voices and the sounds of vowels would all take when voiced or played.

A Japanese researcher, Dr. Masaru Emoto, showed that consciousness and intent changed the shape of water crystals. For example, if one taped the word *love* on a water bottle, the shape of the water crystals would transform into symmetry. At the same time, the word *hate* would show up as deformed and distorted crystals.

Since our bodies are more than 60 percent water, this research shows that thoughts and intent have great potential

1

for transformation and realignment within our own structures. This means that sound healing can be a powerful tool for transformation when sound is linked together with consciousness and intent.

Everyday Sounds

Depending on the consciousness and intent behind it, sound can also be used to create distortions in one's energy field. Do you remember those clips from old movies where you heard the drip, drip, drip of a water faucet that was used to torture prisoners? How about the 4/4 rhythm that politicians and preachers incorporate in their speeches to snare and hold an audience? There are also the broadcasters who air commercials at a much louder volume than the programs that are being aired with them.

In this case, sound is used to manipulate and condition your subconscious to control your behavior. This is done by getting and holding your attention so thoughts of buying a certain product are being implanted in your subconscious. These are all examples of how tones that do not hold specific healing frequencies can be used for distorted reasons as well.

To understand more about how sound affects you, you can play with some simple things around the house you use daily. Allow yourself to sense/feel the different effects that sounds create through your body as you play. For example, when you mess with the television and you get white static noise, what reaction do you sense/feel in your body? When you sit quietly at home and suddenly a noise is made, no matter how low or soft, does it send ripples or waves through your energy template (pattern or blueprint)? For just a few seconds, does it feel like an intrusion of wave interference in your energy template until you balance it out?

Where in the body do you feel the sound? When sound comes through the electrical system, do you perhaps notice it in your head? Not with the ears, but somewhere much deeper in your template? But then as your awareness grows stronger, perhaps the waves seem to expand downward through your template to allow your whole body to hear and feel the wave currents.

Many people have pets, so there might be a constant barking from a house off in the distance. Nighttime insect noises will sometimes be felt as an irritation in your energy fields. The sound of someone clipping their nails can drive people crazy, as it also sends waves of irritation through their templates. Most of the time we simply go about our day and block out those sounds, but when we are quiet, they can become a constant irritation to our fields. In some people, these constant noises can spark a migraine.

People respond to music in different ways as well. Some like it; others consider it noise. For example, some people may like rap or rock music but not classical. Others prefer classical but not rap or rock. Some like all three. It may be the irritation that certain instruments and rhythms cause in those people's energetic template based on longer or shorter waveforms, the speed at which they move through you, and whether those waveforms seem to flow.

For some, stringed instruments seem to create a longer wave, and keyboard instruments seem to create a flowing wave that zigzags through the template. Wind instruments, especially the flute, seem to create a celestial-type wave that takes one higher than any other instrument. Of course, the effects of such waves are different for everyone, so those instruments might not have the same effect on everyone. However, sounds of all kinds do affect our energetic template.

Sound influences every aspect of our lives. We can control some of these influences; others we cannot. If we can understand on some level the power of everyday sound in our environment and the effect it creates in our templates and holograms, then perhaps we will make more aware and conscious choices about the sounds we bring into our environments that we can control. We can make choices about what we want to listen to on television. We can use more soundproofing in our environments. We can actively search out music that makes our bodies feel better, and we can start using our own voices and innate toning abilities to help in our own personal healing journeys.

Something to Ponder: Find a piece of music you enjoy hearing and put it in your player. Sit with that. Put your hands on the playing device and focus on the waves coming out of the device into your home and body. Then change the music and feel again the waves emanating from the player. Try to sense/feel the difference in the waves.

Unheard Sound

In sound and consciousness, we have what I call *unheard sound*. It is sound coming in on a frequency that we do not have the audio receptors to hear, yet we can often feel or sense it. When I have taken hearing tests, there were some sounds I was not sure if I had heard or not. It was like I did not have a really good sense of hearing them, yet something changed when they were emitted. Perhaps it was a change in the air that I felt, or maybe I felt the sound wave itself. Whatever it was, I knew a sound was being emitted.

Our energetic structures, on which our physical bodies are based, are built of sound and light. Even if we cannot hear a sound, it still affects us. Science has shown that sound can both heal and destroy, and the intentional focus of consciousness with sound magnifies the effects. The more we align our consciousness with the wholeness of the Divine Source, the greater our ability to affect others in healing will be. One of the ways we do this is through the silent radiation of sound and light from our biofields. I had a teacher once who said I could get to the point where people could receive healing from just walking through my energy fields. The quality of consciousness, radiating as sound and light, is the key.

Each instance we encounter and our response to those events work in our templates to create the tone we are going to carry into the next moment. Everything we encounter as we travel to work sets our personal tones for when we get to work. We radiate those sounds or tones to others until we clear our templates to allow us to access different tones. We do have the ability and power to change our tones throughout the day. We change our tones by altering our thinking and the emotions behind the thoughts. I may smile outwardly, but if I am feeling resentful or angry inside, then my energy fields will emanate the anger frequency.

Sound is consciousness, but it is also a carrier of consciousness. Whatever I am thinking or feeling goes out on the sound I emanate silently. I carry who I am in every moment, and that consciousness continually radiates out to all with whom I come into contact.

Something to Ponder: Sit or lie down on the ground or on the earth, if your body allows it. If not, then try to place some part of your body on the ground. Make an intention to send a blessing to the earth through the singing or toning of your inner self. Then tone or sing with that intent. When finished, just breathe from your abdomen and feel for the response from the consciousness of the earth. It may come as ripples, waves, or just a sense of knowing or feeling.

The more you do this exercise, the stronger your ability to feel a response will be. Your discernment will strengthen along with your ability to feel waves without hearing a sound.

Consciousness Space of Source

Sound is a carrier of consciousness. Aligning with your concept of the Divine Source and then toning from that consciousness space is a powerful technique for change. During a healing session, I tone this Divine Source frequency whenever my intuition leads me to do so. Using tones in an attitude of Source-centered wholeness allows you to tap into the healing consciousness of the universe, both for yourself and your client.

Toning or chanting from the consciousness space of the Divine Source over a period of time will result in changes within your consciousness. The sounds aligned with this consciousness intent attract the essence of purity to align with the purity of your divine self within. This alignment propels negativity out of your energy fields and brings it forward to the attention of your conscious self for forgiveness and release. We start to bring forth from the universe the knowledge of changing a body's pattern of distortion into one of harmony.

We become creators of form and allow the original blueprint of perfection and wholeness to come forth. When used with intention and an inner focus on wholeness, toning from Divine Source consciousness is a very high spiritual form of healing.

Any healing we hope to facilitate begins first within ourselves. If our thoughts are focused on needing to fix or on judging others as not whole, then any healing we appear to facilitate will only be an illusion and reflects our thoughts about our own state of wholeness. In pondering the concept or feeling of wholeness, we can choose our own symbols or symbolic concepts to align with.

Some of the concepts throughout history include those that denote the wholeness of All There Is or Divine Source emanating from the center of the universe or that which we call the Great Central Sun. Wholeness for some could describe that which births the son/daughter principle and that which the son/daughter principal devolves back into. It could be something that symbolizes the Divine Flame within us all and the power to co-create our reality. Wholeness could also be symbolized by the imagery of a deep pool of still water within, a metaphor for an infinite depth of consciousness available to all. Each person will have a picture or image that works for them.

In aligning with Divine Source consciousness, we allow ourselves to surrender into or merge within the allness of life, the Oneness of the universe. It allows us to find the balance and center in the midst of everyday activity. We become the eye of the storm, the eye of the hurricane.

The purpose for toning sounds from a space of Source consciousness is to help you move from the little will to the Divine Will—from I will this to be done to thy will be done, or Divine Right Order. They allow us to merge with Divine

Timing and Divine Right Action and claim them for both ourselves and our clients.

Co-creating with Divine Source consciousness is very powerful and can aid in opening the spiritual centers in the head and heart, which then can invoke a higher energetic state of consciousness. Therefore, when you first start working with sound and Divine Source consciousness, it can result in a temporary feeling of dizziness.

Grounding is very important here. You should always ground yourself to the earth when working with sound by imagining roots of light extending from one of your energy centers at the solar plexus, your abdomen, or the root of your spine, through your feet into the earth. With consistent use, this will help the dizziness pass.

The Power of Words

Words have a vibration behind and within them. When spoken verbally or silently, they can affect a person's energetic structure based on the intention with which they are spoken. This then becomes the energetic signature or encryption of each word sent forth. This is not only because of the fuller definition a word carries in intent, but also because of the sound tones a word carries. There are words that can express the same desired thought patterns but at a much higher level of frequency because of the sound tones they carry when spoken outward, but also when heard inward, as when reading.

Sound is a creative force. At the beginning of creation, sound is a standing wave of vibration. As this vibration moves within itself, a creative thought aligns with it. Riding this wave, a thought moves out into manifestation, as sound moves out into the creation worlds as light. This light then fills in the template created by the thought. The more consistent thrust or emotion you put behind a thought, the stronger the template and the thought form created. This thought form becomes the operational instructions you give yourself.

This thought form created through sound and light can be thought of as a geometric symbol or code. That is why you have certain languages that do not just have letters, but symbols that equate to total concepts or thoughts. Once again, you have light and sound coming together to form a language for manifestation. This language works whether you speak it mentally or verbally.

This connection of thought to sound is very important. First of all, you have words whose root seems to be in opposition to what the word actually means, for instance, the word *awful*. It means full of awe, highly impressive, or reverential. Yet it also means something bad. This can set up a distorted thought form when consciously you have not realized this conflict in meaning, but subconsciously you have. So it is very important to be aware of the words you are using. There is a consciousness behind the words, and if it is a distorted consciousness, then you are going to create distortion when you use those words.

Second, it is important to make sure you are centered and aligned with the highest consciousness you can because the words you speak are powerful. If a distorted consciousness speaks words that are distorted themselves, then this becomes a very powerful formula for manifesting reversals in both yours and someone else's energy fields.

In the study of cymatics, researchers found that sound creates geometric symbols in sand or liquid. In experiments using Hebrew or Sanskrit, speaking the language actually created the symbol used for certain words. These symbols are thus a visual (light) representation of specific sound tones. These tones and symbols have been used for ages to connect with certain levels of consciousness. This could mean that if the sound tones and symbols become distorted, then the energetic gateways previously created in our energy fields are no longer aligned with our consciousness.

One could theorize that through the misuse of sound and light, your connection with a higher aspect of self could actually be lost. So it is part of your responsibility as a powerful creative being to be aware of the words you use and the thoughts you think—to be mindful at all times of what you are creating in this world.

Something to Ponder: An interesting exercise would be to take a piece of paper with the words you wish to speak or sing written upon it. Then hold the paper close to your face as you sing or tone the sounds. What you might discover are sound tones bouncing back from the paper, moving into your chest area, and, then as your toning increases, filling your body with waves of vibrational tones.

Practice playing with that effect. You might find that you have "aha" moments because the power of consciousness and sound tone vibrations can result in an internalized wave of energy that moves through the body on the sound tone vibrations. An "aha" moment can result from that wave filling your body as your brain becomes aware of whatever truth wants to be heard at that moment.

Voices of Healing

The process of healing used in the chapter on Standing in the Presence is called "speaking your word." This is a very powerful adjunct to healing and can be enhanced by the type of voice used. Three types of voices of healing are mentioned in this chapter: the intellectual voice, the love/wisdom voice, and the power voice. Combining the voices results in a more powerful healing treatment, but they may be used by themselves.

Intellectual Voice

The intellectual voice manifests when you are logically making a point. It has the flavor of "this is all very logical, so of course it will work." It reminds the mental body of its task to come into balance with the physical/etheric, emotional, and spiritual bodies. One must be heart-centered when using the intellectual voice. This allows the speaker to connect with a higher mind and know wholeness for the client. It invites the hearers to participate in consciousness—to create their own reality. The intellectual voice's ability to catalyze healing is degraded when people are centered energetically in the head.

Love/Wisdom Voice

The sound of the love/wisdom voice resonates with the heart center. Your tone of voice implies "there is only love in the universe, and through this love, all is perfect, and all is well." It is a sound of unconditional love that catalyzes a coming into wholeness for many people. Love takes us out of the ego and allows us to hold the door of consciousness open for others to walk through. It speaks to the soul, drawing forth the soul's inherent perfection. Healing, enlightenment, and accelerated spiritual evolution follow.

Power Voice

The sound of the power voice resonates with the power of the heart center connected to the will center (solar plexus chakra). You are essentially saying through your tone of voice, "I declare this to be done but done in Divine Love or Divine Order." It is a sound that matches well with the decrees or I Am statements used in the fourth step of the healing process laid out in the chapter on Standing in the Presence. It tells the universe that the word you are speaking is truth; therefore you have no doubt that the outcome of the healing treatment must be perfection. This is a dynamic voice that helps shatter old thought patterns and build new ones.

Using sound to resonate with the will center does not mean to come from the third chakra. It means essentially you are calling Divine Order into the situation. Start by performing the Tower of Power exercise in the chapter on Expanding Awareness of You as Source. This exercise will balance, center, and open you up to connect you to Source.

Something to Ponder: Once you feel balanced, visualize expanding the energy space within your body. Sense the feeling of expansion. Put your awareness on your total self, the physical center of which is the heart-solar plexus area. Maintain the expanded feeling. Now speak your word, feeling the words resonate within your heart-solar plexus area and expanding out. Let the power radiate, carrying your words with it. The Tower of Power exercise in the final chapter will align your will with the Will of Source. Then when you consciously radiate the power outwardly, you will be standing within your authority as a Spark of Source incarnate, creating with Source energy. It will not be a question of your will dominating a client's will. It will be a case of saying to and within Source, "I will that thy will be my will. The words I speak are Truth and therefore by Universal Law *must* manifest!"

Bringers of Joy

Loving joy is a wonderful energy that you can allow to flow out on the sounds you make. It is a consciousness that is very healing because it is the consciousness of the Divine Source. When you build an inner pillar filled with the loving joy of Source, you start radiating these sound and light waves into the planet's template and all levels of creation, setting that pattern within all reality fields. It is a simple process you can initiate via what we call the "individual loving joy memory moment."

Because of the diversity of DNA coding, it could be a reason why different people are attracted to various types of songs. This would include different sound sequences and rhythms, along with quite possibly different types of instruments. Therefore, certain people might be attracted to classical music and others to jazz, pop, rock, and so forth. The more diverse your template coding, the more you would enjoy different styles/types of music or a fusion of styles (pop rock, classical pop, etc.)

What does this mean for us at this time? Each of us is a diverse world within ourselves. We each bring a hybrid of coding from all parts of a multitude of universes. When we sing through, and as our authentic core self, then the genetic race lines connected to these codes receive the consciousness sent out on the song and, to the extent they are able, realign to the wholeness inherent within the song(s). Even singing silently with all the authenticity we hold at any moment of time will start the healing, the coming into wholeness for whoever can hear at that moment.

Loving Joy Song

Loving joy songs, those that reflect our personal frequency, will start this process. The frequency of the song combines with that of the singer, fusing the two to produce a specific energetic spectrum. The artist then is as crucial as the song. Important too is the version, as one piece might not carry the full spectrum of frequency desired, even if sung by the same person.

The songs that allow us to feel as if we are overflowing with the loving joy of the Divine Source hold specific sound tones that we are keyed to. Creation is made of harmonics of sound. When we listen to a song that helps us feel the loving joy within, we first hear the harmonics of the notes played. Then we hear and sense energetic peak points within those harmonics that seem to lift us up even higher energetically. If we sing along, we might sing louder, put more strength into our voice, and possibly move our bodies faster at these peak points.

These songs, propelled by the consciousness we hold, are sent out into the world on the sound wave and manifest as the light within all creation. The understanding of diversity and how it contributes to a whole will unify the pillar you build. Knowing that through our diversity there is wholeness, as we sing the loving joy songs, a pillar will form within ourselves, filled with the loving joy of the Divine Source.

This pillar, sung into creation via each individual loving joy memory moment, will form part of a group pillar template. This group pillar template formed of sound and light waves will be amplified through the loving joy songs and then radiated from our individual and group consciousness out into the planetary consciousness and all levels of creation to set that pattern.

Key to this process of radiating joy is the ability to relax and have fun with friends and family. Fun is like the on-ramp onto the freeway of joy. So as we breathe, we can allow this divine joy energy to fill our templates. Then we open our mouths and sing our soul sounds, allowing ourselves to play with the sound tones, trying different sounds and rhythms. We can close our eyes and sense/feel the tones and rhythms flowing through our bodies. We can dance and move as the Spirit leads us and just be the joyous, radiant beings we are and always were.

From this center of joy, we sing the joy songs. We can sing out in the joy and understanding of why we are here at this moment in space-time. We can move into our center of wholeness/holiness and radiate a new probability through the consciousness we hold.

Reconnecting with the Loving Joy Feeling of Source

We have the opportunity at this moment in time to birth a new pattern of consciousness. We have the opportunity to birth authenticity, clarity, grace, love, and, of course, joy as well as all the facets of the Divine Source consciousness we can hold in that shining singing moment. We are, and will be, bringers of joy.

We are made of light and sound, and through the interaction of light and sound, we create our reality, give instructions to our energetic body, and communicate with our multidimensional family and the Divine Source. We have an entire spectrum of light and sound available to assist us in reconnecting with the loving joy feeling of the Divine Source. This connection of the light and sound within us, by helping us reconnect with the loving joy feeling of the Divine Source, can assist us to talk to, listen to, and heal our emotional body while making a stronger connection to the Divine Source.

A Loving Joy Thought Memory

The first step is to find a loving joy memory. Some might have to look deeper than others to find a loving joy memory, but it is in you somewhere. It could be a memory of finding new love, holding that newborn baby in your arms for the first time, getting married, having an exceptionally strong communication with Source, or simply viewing a breathtaking image that the earth presents us with. Try locating a memory held within yourself that with each remembrance brings to you a complete overfilled-with-love feeling, a memory that will always remain one of your most precious recollections.

When you have located your memory, hold that experience in your head, in your focused now moment thought. Allow yourself to relive that memory in your mind. See the surroundings, the environment the memory occurred within. Was it inside or outside? Was it day or night? What was the weather like: sunny, rainy, warm, or cold? Allow yourself to feel and see the weather of that moment.

See the surroundings of the loving joy experience. If inside, see the furnishings, the things hanging on the walls, and the floor beneath your feet. What does the floor feel like beneath your feet? Go outside and try to re-create the exact same surrounding in your mind. Feel the air on your skin or the warmth of the sun, if it is shining.

Hear the sounds from your stored memory. Was there music playing? Were other people talking? Was there noise from auto traffic around you? Did you eat food in your stored loving joy moment? If so, try to see the food and remember the tastes and smells as they moved over your tongue.

Allow yourself to fully emerge yourself in that stored

memory. Then pay attention to the emotions that were running through your body at that moment in time. The love you feel in that moment may be so strong to allow tears to fall now, as you re-create that moment in your mind. That is wonderful if it does because that means you are fully reconnecting with that stored loving joy memory.

Once you can reconnect with the stored emotions of that moment, allow yourself to sit with those emotions. Allow your physical body to completely feel all of those loving feelings all over again. Those feelings of being filled to overflowing with love are the loving joy of the Divine Source.

We can only experience a tiny spark of the full expression of the loving joy of the Divine Source in our physical body as the full expression would be so strong, it would blow up our physical body. This feeling is the one that the Divine Source creates all of creation eternally. Because we are eternal, we never run out of time to heal. Source gifts us with a huge amount of the loving joy of the Divine Source to allow us an opportunity to heal.

The feeling of the loving joy of the Divine Source will continue to grow and expand within us as we heal. If we allow it, we can begin to remember the absolute joy of viewing and experiencing the world through the eyes of innocence. This is the Divine Source energy that our newly written script, through our thoughts and feelings, will carry into our reality, and we, as the script writers, can fill in that script with whatever we desire to experience.

If we co-create through the emotional feelings of the loving joy of the Divine Source, we will discover that those types of experiences, that may now seem to be far and few between, increase. This same energy will allow your emotional body to heal, and we can use specific sound tones individually keyed to us to assist this process.

Something to Ponder: For this moment, talk to your inner child. Thank your inner child for holding on to that wonderful, loving joy moment for you.

Something to Ponder: Think about your relationship with the inner you and how the inner you sustains you, loves you, and is a focal point for healing. How might you co-create healing with your inner self?

The Power of Encryption

We are literally swimming within a sea of energy. It is impossible not to be within a sea of energy because all of creation is taking place within the conscious, energetic mind of Divine Source. However, there are different levels of seas of energy within Divine Source. We might compare these different levels to puddles, creeks, streams, lakes, rivers, and oceans. Each sea of energy will carry stronger energy thrusts as waves ripple through.

Similar to swimming within the fluid inside the womb of our mothers, when we leave that sea, we slip out of that environment into a much larger sea. Of course, we were already in that much larger sea within the womb as well. This helps us to understand that our view of creation is only limited by our current-moment focus of our environment. When we become aware of more of the truth of the larger environment we exist within, it allows us to understand more about ourselves and creation through greater expansion of thought.

Our bodies continue to pick up on all of the effects of unheard and unseen sound and light patterns throughout life, just like the baby growing inside the mother's womb can pick up on everything outside of the mother's womb. Once birthed, we are still within an energetic environment that is bombarded with sound and light. This bombardment happens even if we cannot hear the sound with our ears or see the light with our eyes.

We pick up on sounds in many other ways than simply hearing them with our ears. We pick up sound vibrations with our entire physical/emotional/energetic body anatomy. Have you ever pulled up beside a car at a stoplight and the driver of the car is playing their music through bass speakers that creates a wave of energy that not only vibrates their car but yours as well? You may have your windows rolled up and not even be able to hear their music, but your body can still feel the vibrations of the sound.

Many people have most likely heard of subliminal sound programming. Department stores used to use this technology years ago to cut down on shoplifting. There are also dog whistles that emit a sound that is out of the range of human hearing, but dogs can hear it, and they do not like it. It creates an irritation to their ears.

Experiments and studies have been conducted on the effects of different sounds on the fetus in the womb. Such experiments and studies suggest that when stress from the environment and expectant mother is balanced, then a developing fetus will be calmer and happier. Many expectant mothers will play soft, soothing music against their stomach so the child growing within can hear and be calmed. They know the child growing within can also hear every thought the mother has, every word spoken, and every emotional reaction the mother carries.

Sounds, words, and the encryptions or mathematical programs they carry can shape or mold everything we choose to believe is truth. A child subjected to an environment in which they are constantly told they are bad will grow into an adult who believes they are terrible. They will portray a personality in which they outwardly express everything that they hold true about themselves.

We are made of light and sound, and because we are individuated faces of the Divine Source, we each carry specific sound tones that are keyed specifically to our energetic body.

Depending on what vibration those sound tones carry, these individual sound tones will give specific instructions to our energetic body. As a result, some people thrive in an environment in which they need to play different types of music in order to concentrate. Some require soft, soothing music; others need loud music. And many require the noise of a television. Others simply need quiet and the listening to their own thoughts.

When we encounter sound tones that our energetic body is keyed to, we like those sound tones and want to hear them again and again. But when we encounter sound tones that our energetic body is not keyed to, we want to shut them off or get away from them immediately. They create an irritation in our physical and energetic bodies, like fingernails on a chalkboard.

Each individual has their own unique energetic wiring. Some people are more sensitive to sounds than others are, and the sensory impact of different sounds and rhythms can impact how they approach life. The key point is to learn to pay attention to how the different sounds and light affect us and perhaps make notes of these effects. We can thus find a pattern of what would work best for each of us in our effort to co-create more balance within our personal lives.

When we take time to recognize the environment we are living within affects our body and thoughts, we can become more in tune to our body's responses. This will allow us to begin to notice when something is heightened in our environment and affecting us, even though we might not be able to see or hear it. This is the beginning process of remembering how we are affected consistently by waves of energy that eternally move through our reality field and our bodies.

We can change what we are allowing ourselves to believe to be truth simply by remembering how to pay attention to our thoughts and words. Thoughts and words are light and sound patterns that are continually giving operational instructions to our body, including the brain. We are the manifesters of all the experiences in our daily lives. If we constantly tell ourselves the opposite of what we actually desire to experience, that is exactly what we experience, and we will never experience what we actually desire. We do not allow ourselves to because we are constantly telling ourselves we will not or cannot have it.

We are experiencing life within a world where humans are keyed to a fast-paced environment. Go, go, go, go, go. Always on the move to get ahead, make more money, see more things, and have more experiences, and as we do so, we give very little attention to the thoughts that stream through our brains nonstop.

We give very little attention to the words that come out of our mouths. We are currently programmed to speak in slang or even letters that do not even spell a word but have become an accepted encryption, and lots of people simply know what is meant because of those few little letters. Did you know that LOL means "laughing out loud" in the United States, but "lots of love" in the United Kingdom?

The physical brain and the entire body are easily programmed with our thoughts, sounds, light, and energy. Light and sound are the tools by which we create everything we will experience in our daily lives. We may not currently be aware of all of the different types of waves of energy in creation that express as either light or sound, but that does not mean we are not affected by them.

The Divine Source creates all of creation simply through the aspects of light and sound and the way they will interact with each other. Yes, that means our solid, manifest body is made of light and sound. The way we tell our bodies and ourselves how to operate is through the energy of light and sound. Knowing that, it then becomes very beneficial to become aware of exactly what instructions we are giving to our bodies.

Other Life-forms

All life-forms respond to sound. Plants respond to loving, gentle kind words. They thrive better in such an environment versus one in which there is constant yelling or arguing. It is not just the sounds that have an impact on the plant, but also the conscious thoughts being pushed forth into the environment. One could use words that carry known lower vibrational encryptions such as "I hate you" and yet speak with the same voice tones that to the ear sounds like you are saying, "I love you." Though the tones may sound the same, the person saying the words knows the difference in the meaning of the words, and they will send forth on the sound tones the encrypted meaning as energy expanding from their body.

Both the sound tones and the encryption will affect the plant. So you could talk to your philodendron plant every day in a gentle, soothing voice while repeating and thinking the words "I hate you," and your plant would most likely die very quickly.

Pets are calmed very quickly by gentle, soothing music and most likely will go to sleep, whereas louder noises and something like rock-and-roll music will excite them quickly. They will go about their natural ways of making more noise and being more excited. Dogs especially will bark loudly at loud sounds, such as loud trucks or gunshots, and some dogs will even chase vehicles. I have always wondered what the dog thought it might do if it ever actually caught one of the vehicles. Most often it is the annoying sounds the vehicle makes that annoys the dog.

Something to Ponder: Think for a moment of all the sounds you are bombarded with daily. Some of the sounds that come to mind might be the refrigerator, air-conditioner, washing machine and dryer, cars, police sirens, dogs barking, or babies crying. Start paying attention to how your body and emotions react in your personal sonic environment.

Something to Ponder: What can you do to alleviate some or all of the stress that various sounds cause in your body? What can you do to alleviate or decrease emotional reactions to different sounds in your environment?

Something to Ponder: Is there a way to use sound to bring peace and balance into your daily living environment?

Consciousness and Healing Bowls

Sound breaks up patterns of energy and allows the body the opportunity to manifest its original soul blueprint. When the body holds life-denying patterns of energy, sound will assist in penetrating and dissolving the energy armor. Outmoded patterns can then be lifted out and the resulting space infused with Divine Source energy. Sound in partnership with any modality increases the effectiveness of the modality and facilitates smoother levels of change.

What is sound? What we perceive as a single tone is in reality a mixture of tone frequencies or pitches. Pitch is the result of vibration—how fast sound, taking the form of waves, vibrates. We measure sound waves in units called hertz (Hz). Hertz is the measure we use for the number of cycles per second the waves create. Therefore, a string that vibrates back and forth 256 times a second when played creates a sound whose frequency is 256 Hz, and we name it middle C.

When an instrument is played, what sounds to us like a single note is actually a combination of harmonic overtones. Very rarely does an instrument produce a single, pure tone. The lowest frequency we hear is how we define the note. If I play a crystal bowl or instrument that is tuned in the key of C, it means C is the lowest frequency. The other tone frequencies, overtones, contribute to the specific voice or sound color of an instrument. All instruments have overtones, but specific dominant overtones within each instrument give it a unique personality.

Crystal Bowls Are Alive

All life has consciousness. When we look at a crystal or Tibetan bowl, we may think they are inanimate, but if we believe that all creation comes from and out of a creator or Divine Source, who is pure consciousness, then those bowls by default have consciousness and are conscious on some level.

When we play with sound, we are co-creating with a force that is both playful and powerful. In many creation stories, you hear that in the beginning was sound, and when it moved and projected out into manifestation, it became light. Light subsequently slowed down its rotation of particle spin and became matter. This concept gives us a wonderful visual for playing with both sound and light.

Play Time

It is time to play. Sit down comfortably on the floor or pillow and place the crystal bowl on the floor in front of you. Allow your hands to fold loosely on your lap.

1. Close your eyes and take several deep breaths to relax and center yourself. Slow the breath, making sure you breathe from your abdomen. As you expand your abdomen, allow the breath to also expand your diaphragm and lungs in conjunction with it. Breathe in and allow the breath to flow to all areas of your body, and as you exhale, breathe out all the tension you have accumulated. Inhale ... hold ... breathe out as you mentally say "I am relaxed. I am peace. I am Divine Source now. I am One with All There Is now."

2. Build your pillar of sound-light. You can do this either mentally or with actual sound, toning as you imagine a pillar of sound-light reaching up to Source and down to the center of the earth where you connect via your earth star chakra.

3. Connect with the consciousness of the bowl. Ask it to co-create with you through and from its original Divine Blueprint. Ask permission from the bowl to place your hands on it and play it. If you sense/feel/hear the answer is no, then honor that.

4. If you sense/feel/hear a yes, then with great reverence, place your hands upon the bowl and begin to play. Tap the bowl with a padded striker three times to start the sound vibrating. Then drag the padded end of the striker around the outside rim of the bowl. Press slightly against the bowl to create resistance. The degree of loudness of the sound will depend on how firmly you press the striker against the bowl. As you play, lift your hands periodically to allow the sound to rise; otherwise the sound could get trapped inside the bowl and cause the bowl to implode.

5. Continue to play, relaxing into a state of aware conscious co-creation. You may sense/feel an increase, like a crescendo of energy, in the wave of sound pouring out. Eventually you will have a sense of completion. This is where you stop and lay your hands down once more in your lap.

6. Allow yourself to close your eyes and relax into a sense of stillness and wholeness. Breathe softly into your pillar, and send a mental "thank you" to the consciousness of the bowl and to Source. Make sure your pillar is grounded down into earth core. Then take a few more breaths to ensure you are fully in body before you get up.

Non-local Healing with the Bowls

Non-local healing is a term often used interchangeably with distant healing. In the realm of Spirit, time and distance do not exist. Therefore, non-local and present healing treatments are the same. Because there is no separation in the field of universal mind and spirit, when we speak our word or send our word out on the sound currents, we do this in full confidence that our word has power. We then release the thought into the unified field, into universal mind, which then reacts to our belief. This all happens, not somewhere else, but in the Absolute Now. Thus, in the consciousness of the healing practitioner, giving a distance healing treatment means the same thing as giving a present treatment.

The following technique for non-local healing is a way for our creative consciousness and the consciousness of the crystal bowl to form a space of universal Divine Order and healing. It is a divine partnership based on the concept that all is of the One Presence, the One Divine Source, and all is happening in the present, the Absolute Now.

1. Close your eyes and take several deep breaths to relax and center yourself. Slow the breath, making sure you breathe from your abdomen. As you expand your abdomen, allow the breath to also expand your diaphragm and lungs in conjunction with it. Breathe in and allow the breath to flow to all areas of your body, and as you exhale, you breathe out all the tension you have accumulated. Inhale ... hold ... breathe out as you mentally say "I am relaxed. I am peace. I am Divine Source now; I am One with All There Is now."

2. Continue to breathe in the energy of the Divine Source. Become the in-breath and out-breath of Divine Source to the point of knowing ... and recognizing ... there is only Divine Source and the coming into union with Source.

3. Build your pillar of sound-light. You can do this either mentally or with actual sound.

4. Connect with the consciousness of the bowl. Ask it to co-create with you through and from its original Divine Blueprint.

5. Visualize the bowl as a golden-silver pattern or matrix of light. Visualize yourself as a matrix or pattern of light. And let the two patterns or matrices come together and form a partnership pattern in Divine Right Order.

6. Ask permission from the bowl to place your hands on it and play it. If you sense/feel/hear the answer is no, then honor that.

7. If you sense/feel/hear a yes, then with great reverence, place your hands upon the bowl and begin to play. Tap the bowl with a padded striker three times to start the sound vibrating. Then drag the padded end of the striker around the outside rim of the bowl two or three times.

8. Do invocational prayer treatments, declarative intentions, spiritual mind treatments, I Am statements, or other forms of affirmative statements or prayers (spoken, toned, sung, or chanted).

9. Begin to play the bowl once again. Press slightly against the bowl to create resistance. The degree of loudness of the sound will depend on how firmly you press the striker against the bowl. As you play, lift your hands periodically to allow the sound to rise; otherwise the sound could get trapped inside the bowl and cause the bowl to implode.

10. Continue to play, relaxing into a state of aware conscious co-creation. You may sense/feel an increase, like a crescendo of energy, in the wave of sound pouring out. Eventually you will have a sense of completion. This is where you stop and lay your hands down once more in your lap.

11. Allow yourself to close your eyes and relax into a sense of stillness and wholeness. Breathe softly into your pillar, and send a mental "thank you" to the consciousness of the bowl. Make sure your pillar is grounded down into earth core. Then take a few more breaths to ensure you are fully in body before you get up.

Note: It is very important to ask permission of a person before you perform any healing for them. Otherwise, it is considered a violation of spiritual integrity. Permission can be obtained in two ways. The first is by actually speaking to the person. The second, which is often used in cases of extreme illness, after a traumatic accident, or while a person is in the process of dropping the body (dying), is to center yourself, connect with the Higher Self of the person, and ask the Higher Self. If you get a no, honor that. Whatever process the person is going through is what they and their Higher Self are orchestrating for their own growth or because it is time to drop the body and they do not want anything to interfere with that process. Sometimes they will give assent for your assistance even if the person is in the process of dropping the body because they may want energetic help on a certain level to ease or accelerate the process. If you feel an assent has been given, make sure you ask several times to make sure your ego does not feel the need to help, but is a true request.

Sound Is Consciousness

Sound is consciousness, and consciousness travels on sound. So it is very important when using sound to be in a state of wholeness consciousness. Wholeness consciousness is a state where you feel, sense, or see yourself as whole and unbroken. It is a state where you are totally healed. You would align yourself with wholeness consciousness because it is the original state you were in when Source created you. It is the consciousness state of Divine Right Order.

The focus on Divine Right Order becomes the operational instructions you give your inner core self and, through you, to the client's core self. It makes no difference whether the facilitator uses the voice, orchestral instruments, or crystal/ Tibetan bowls. This state of consciousness, where the healing facilitator has an inner focus on wholeness, the original Divine Blueprint, or divine perfection, will be what travels out on the sound as the facilitator generates or voices the sound.

Something to Ponder: Try keeping an inner focus on wholeness throughout the day. The more you practice, the more consistent you will be in maintaining a state of wholeness consciousness throughout the sound healing treatment.

Something to Ponder: Think about the concept of Divine Right Order. If your inner focus is on Divine Right Order, how might that affect you on a daily basis? How might that affect your client during a healing session?

Consciousness and Percussion
in Sound Healing

Consciousness of Sound and Rhythm

All life has consciousness. When we look at a drum, rattle, marimba, claves, and so on, we may think they are inanimate. However, all creation comes from and out of a creator or Divine Source who is pure consciousness. Therefore, these percussion instruments by default have consciousness and are conscious on some level.

When we play with rhythm and sound, we are co-creating with forces that are both playful and powerful. In many creation stories, you hear that in the beginning was sound, and when it moved and projected out into manifestation, it became light. Light subsequently slowed down its rotation of particle spin and became matter. So light and sound become matter, but rhythm determines the shape it takes.

Play Time

It is time to play. Sit down comfortably on the floor or pillow and just allow your hands to fold loosely on your lap. If you choose to stand, slightly bend your knees, flexing them a bit, and allow your hands to hang loosely at your sides.

1. Slow the breath, making sure you breathe from your abdomen. As you expand your abdomen, allow the breath to also expand your diaphragm and lungs in conjunction with it. Breathe in and allow the breath to flow to all areas

of your body, and as you exhale, you breathe out all the tension you have accumulated. Inhale ... hold ... breathe out as you mentally decree "I am relaxed. I am peace. I am Divine Source now. I am One with All There Is now."

2. Build your pillar of sound-light. You can do this either mentally or with actual sound/toning/singing. Continue to breathe, this time imagining a silver-white color to the breath.

3. Connect with the consciousness of your instrument. Ask it to co-create with you through and from its original Divine Blueprint. Ask permission from the instrument to place your hands on it and play it. If you sense/feel/hear the answer is no, then honor that.

4. If you sense/feel/hear a yes, then with great reverence, place your hands upon the drum or pick up your mallets/drumsticks/rattles and begin to play.

5. Begin by beating a heartbeat rhythm as a baseline. This will serve to entrain your brain to a basic life beat, which your consciousness and body will be aware of and serve as a rhythmic foundation when you start to move into other rhythms.

6. Do not predetermine any specific rhythms as you start to improvise. The object is to find out what and how the instrument wants to create.

7. Maintain an inner focus on your pillar while allowing your hands to follow the rhythm that wants to appear and co-create in your hologram.

8. Listen with your whole body. Sense/feel any knowing that arises. Sense that the instrument is creating its own pillar of sound-light. Then allow yourself to co-create a group pillar with your sound instrument.

9. Continue to play, relaxing into a state of aware conscious co-creation. You may sense/feel an increase, like a crescendo of energy, in the wave of sound pouring out. You may find yourself moving from rhythmic pattern to rhythmic pattern.
10. Continue to focus on the stillness within. Allow the consciousness of your hands to direct the instrument. They know what to do if you allow it.
11. Allow the continuous alignment with Divine Source. The result will be the original divine intent of Source flowing out on and through the rhythm of the sound.
12. Eventually you will have a sense of completion. This is where you stop and lay your hands down once more in your lap or by the sides of your body.
13. Allow yourself to close your eyes and relax into a sense of stillness and wholeness. Breathe softly into your pillar, and send a mental "thank you" to the consciousness of the instruments. Make sure your pillar is grounded down into earth core. Then take a few more breaths to ensure you are fully in body before you get up.

Drumming the Healing

Allow yourself to play with the drumming so you learn to develop your sense/feeling of co-creating with Divine Source consciousness as you and the drum/rattle. This is the first step in using percussive instruments in sound healing.

In some societies, a sick person is placed in a circle of drummers, or a circle of dancers use their feet as mallets to drum rhythms on the earth. In others, one person will dance, drum, or use a rattle around a sick person to break up stuck energies and restore their life rhythms. This is where it is important to have an inner focus on wholeness. When drumming or dancing around a person, the pattern of the rhythms will have a cleansing effect, going directly into the energy fields. The state of consciousness of the drummers/rattlers/dancers can either help harmonize, heal, and soothe or have an opposite effect on the mind, body, and spirit levels.

Rhythm and Consciousness

All life has its own inherent rhythm. In a sense, you could say that illness results when your own inner rhythm is off track. We use percussive instruments to bring back and repattern your own life rhythm.

The patterns sound makes in an energy field will differ depending on the rhythm and the consciousness behind it. Therefore, it is very important when using sound to be in a state of wholeness consciousness. This state of consciousness, where the healing facilitator has an inner focus on wholeness, the original divine perfection, and the divine rhythm, will be what travels out on the sound as the facilitator plays. This is where alignment with the original rhythmic intention of the Divine Source begins.

Something to Practice: An important step in becoming a sound healer is to activate your innate ability to hear consciousness. An easy way to become familiar with this practice is to hold an instrument in your lap. Focus on it, touch it, ponder what it does and how it sounds, and its potential for healing. As you do this focusing technique, you will begin to find yourself stroking the instrument and becoming one with it. As you continue, create a dialogue with it and listen to its answers. Let it speak through you as it knows its job better than anyone else. It is possible to communicate with any consciousness!

The Body as a Resonating Chamber

Instrument Bodies

Musical instruments such as violins have sound boxes or resonating chambers, where sound waves generated by the musician oscillate in an enclosed space. Therefore, sound resonates to the listener. When a person tones sounds, the physical body as the instrument can act as a resonating chamber.

In teaching voice, we usually think of sound resonating in the head, chest, or throat, supported by diaphragmatic breathing. However, in using toning within sound healing, we want to view sound as resonating within the entire body.

Process

1. Take a moment and start to breathe from your abdomen, expanding your diaphragm at the same time. As you breathe, imagine that other colors are coming in on the breath. I like to imagine I am breathing a mix of silver and white. Then I add others such as gold, aqua, emerald green, or teal, whatever colors come to mind in that moment. Be aware you are breathing frequency.

2. As you breathe, imagine the colored light coming in is expanding the inner part of your body. Everything inside is dissolving to become a column or pillar of light.

3. Expand this inner pillar up to the Divine Source and down to the earth core. Allow it to expand out and up as far as it wants. Then begin to breathe in the frequency of the pillar and on the exhale. Breathe out into the pillar. As

you breathe, be aware of yourself as a spark of the Divine Source. The concept is to not only be a pillar of sound-light, but to be as Source, emanating divine consciousness through sound and light.

4. Begin to tone. I use an *aah* because in my experience, this sound seems to make it easier to open up, expand, and ground the inner pillar. However, feel free to use any vowel sound you feel comfortable with. As you tone, imagine the sounds flowing down into your body as the pillar. Allow these sounds to resonate via the entire body into your pillar of sound-light.

5. Imagine that your body-pillar is emanating this sound 360 degrees around your physical body to help connect it to the physical body-pillar. The goal here is full-body cellular sound emanation. You start with imagining the body emitting sound and then progress to where you can imagine every cell of the body emanating sound.

6. Try to isolate the sound to different parts of your body. Imagine the sound traveling down your right leg and then your left. Sense/feel it now in your right arm and then your left. Sense/feel it now through your central vertical column. Now expand out once again to sense the sound resonating throughout the entire pillar.

7. Bring the processes together. Tone using your entire body as a resonating chamber while at the same time imagining you are sending sound toward different areas of the body.

Something to Practice: Practice this process until you can use the entire body as a resonating/sound chamber and sense/feel the sound through your entire structure. Using your creative imagination will give your body and consciousness the operational instructions to master the process.

Sound and Color Wash

Color is sound made visible. Sound is light made audible. Therefore, light and sound are the same in that they are vehicles of conscious information and information consciousness. We just use different organs of perception to perceive their frequencies and translate the information they carry. We function much like a radio, tuning our senses to pick up frequencies on multi-levels. Those frequencies of light we pick up visually we call color. Those we pick up audibly we call sound.

Another way to look at it is sound as vibration and color as light. Creation starts as a standing wave of vibration (sound) that becomes light when it starts to move out into manifestation. This light then accretes upon and fills out the templates formed through sound, becoming matter.

When light hits the earth, we may see it in its original golden-silvery white color or split into different fragments. These fragments we call wavelengths of color. If you take a prism and hold it up to a source of light such as the sun, you will see the separated colors of the rainbow streaming out. Conversely, upon removing the source of light, the colors move back into a unity of white light.

Einstein's formula for light states energy equals mass times velocity squared, velocity meaning how quickly something moves. Vibration can also be defined as a rapid rhythmic movement back and forth. One could then say that a person's energy depends on how rapid the atomic structure of the body is moving in its prescribed patterns. Therefore, if we could increase the rate of motion of the atomic structure, the rate of vibration would increase, multiplying the energy output of the body.

The traumas you experience and how you perceive and respond to life can decrease the ability of your physical, emotional, mental, and spiritual bodies to function and pull in information from the higher spiritual levels. Thought linked with emotion equals manifestation. Negative thinking therefore takes the basic love energy of the universe and creates it into dense vibrations we name as resentment, anger, fear, and other emotions we categorize as negative or life denying. This chaotic energy becomes part of our personal energy fields and determines what kind of people, relationships, and events we attract into our lives. It is therefore imperative we purify our energy to allow for greater aspects of the God force to manifest in our lives.

Color can be used to create greater harmony on all levels, especially on the emotional level. If an area of our energy usually shines as a bright green but our emotional state has been one of envy, we will re-create and densify the bright green into a dull, sickly yellow-green. Bringing the bright-green wavelength into the aura using candles, colored slides, green clothing, or a heart-centered visualization of green carried on sound waves will assist the person in returning to the original state of bright green. Balance is thereby achieved.

Consciousness and Color

Sound and color have an indelible connection. In the beginning was the word—sound—and Source consciousness moved within itself as a standing wave of sound. When sound began to move into form, it manifested as light. This light differentiated itself within each dimension as different frequency bands of light with different wavelengths of color.

Color has consciousness. Color is light and comes in through our inner vertical connection to Source. When we look at colors, we may think they are inanimate, but if we believe that all creation comes from and out of a creator or Divine Source who is pure consciousness, then color by default is consciousness and also serves as a carrier of consciousness.

When we play with color, we are co-creating with a force that is alive, playful, and powerful. In many creation stories, you hear that in the beginning was sound, and when it moved and projected out into manifestation, it became light. Light subsequently slowed down its rotation of particle spin and became matter. This concept gives us a wonderful visual for playing with light and color in partnership with sound.

Ways to Co-create with Color

The first time I heard about using color with sound was in my voice class in 1976. My teacher had us envision a color and then sing a song as we tried to imbue the song with the feeling of that color. The rest of the class had to try to guess what color the singer was concentrating on. She called this practice "coloring our sound." Later on, I was in a bookstore and found a book about breathing color. It talked about imagining certain colors coming in on the breath as you consciously inhaled. Then you sent the colors to certain areas of your body on the exhale.

You can use this same concept when co-creating a sound healing session with a client. The key, as always, is alignment with and as the Divine Source. Then you mentally call on the consciousness of color to come co-create and play with you.

Steps to Sounding Color

1. Slow the breath, making sure you breathe from your abdomen. As you expand your abdomen, allow the breath to also expand your diaphragm and lungs in conjunction with it. Breathe in and allow the breath to flow to all areas of your body, and as you exhale, you breathe out all the tension you have accumulated. Inhale … hold … breathe out as you mentally say "I am relaxed. I am peace. I am Divine Source now. I am One with All There Is now."

2. Build your pillar of sound-light. You can do this either mentally or with actual sound.

3. Connect with the consciousness of color. Ask it to co-create with you through and from its original divine blueprint. Then move to stand about three feet in back of the head of the client.

4. Start toning. Relax your brain and allow the different colors that want to be part of the healing to flow in on the sound. Imagine these colors and any other effects like glitters, opalescence, or shimmers/sparkles to be part of the co-creative endeavor.

5. Continue to tone, relaxing into a state of aware, conscious co-creation. Allow the colors going out on the sound to flow into the central vertical column. Imagine the colors spreading out into a column or sheet of color that becomes a color wash moving through the body.

6. The color wash cleanses everything in its path and moves out any leftover energetic particles. Set the intent that the color wash will transform those particles into Divine Source energy. Imagine this happening as the color wash moves through the biofields.

7. Eventually you will have a sense of completion. This is when you stop.

8. Allow yourself to close your eyes and relax into a sense of stillness and wholeness. Breathe softly into your pillar, and send a mental "thank you" to the Divine Source.

9. Send a thought of appreciation and gratitude to the consciousness of the colors you co-created with.

10. Make sure your pillar is grounded down into the earth core. Take a few more breaths to ensure you are fully in body before you move.

Play

Do not forget to play and have fun when you co-create with color. There is a joy aspect to helping others remember their wholeness during a healing session. Playing and co-creating with color can help you access that joy and bring healing with sound and color to a whole new level.

Healing Stance

Any true healing practice starts with the practitioner coming from a place of wholeness and stillness within. Sound is a carrier of consciousness, but also sound is consciousness. If I come from that place within where I feel *at-One-ment* or aligned with the Divine Source, where I know myself as whole, then the sound coming out of my mouth will have that same consciousness of wholeness. That is where true healing begins.

Thoughts are very powerful and, coupled with feelings, will create and imprint themselves on a person's energy field. The imprinting becomes an encryption through which a person will operate. Encryptions become the lens through which a person will perceive life and drive the reaction to life's challenges.

Therefore, it is very important for a practitioner to maintain an alignment with an inner picture or sense/feeling of wholeness. The intent of aligning with a sense of wholeness along with maintaining a consciousness of wholeness within will allow the client's energy to come into resonance with the higher frequency of consciousness held by the practitioner.

In a healing session, the client opens their energy field to healing. If the practitioner's focus is not on a connection to Source or wholeness, then the client's open energy field can be overlaid or encrypted with distortions coming from the practitioner's thought and energy patterns. These distortions become a type of operational instruction, directing the client's energy system to run in ways not always for their highest good. The client trusts the practitioner to come from a thought and emotional state of wholeness during the session. Anything less can be considered energetic malpractice.

Question: How do we get into a state of feeling or sensing of wholeness within one's self?

We want to feel a sense of inner unification, a connection to the place where knowing resides. We do not want to get caught up in a thinking process because our energy flows out to the past (what might have happened) or the future (what will happen). We want to stay in the moment, in the Now Point, where cognition and knowingness appear and open the door to healing. One of the best ways to be in this place is through the breath.

The breath is the beginning of movement. Movement of

sound in toning is carried on the breath. The body must be relaxed and able to expand in order to get the full range of sound necessary for sound healing. It is important for energy not to get stuck, and conscious breathing is a great way to propel the energy into movement and a way to keep the energy flowing.

Using the Breath

The first step in using the breath is to slow your breathing, making sure you breathe from your abdomen. As you expand your abdomen, you allow the breath to also expand your diaphragm and lungs in conjunction with it. You breathe in and allow the breath to flow to all areas of your body, and as you exhale, you breathe out all the tension you have accumulated.

Inhale … hold … breathe out as you mentally say "I am relaxed." Other terms you could add depending on your cultural preferences could be "I am whole now. I am Divine Source now. I am One with All There Is now."

Exercise: Let us practice some abdominal/diaphragmatic breathing.

1. Lie on the floor facing up. If you cannot lie down, then sit in a chair, trying not to slump if physically possible.
2. If lying down, bend your knees slightly to allow your lower back to relax against the floor.
3. Relax the abdomen.
4. Place your hands on the area of your body just below the bottom of the rib cage, the location of the diaphragmatic muscle.

5. Expand the body beneath your hands as you inhale, using the expanding of the abdomen to draw in air through the nose. (Think of a baby lying down with its natural abdominal breathing.)

6. As you breathe, allow the expansion of the breath in the abdomen to flow around and expand the area beneath your back, just above the waist (area of the kidneys). Imagine pressing that area into the floor/back of chair with the breath.

7. If you try to consciously take breaths through the nose in order to then expand the abdomen, it will not work very well, and you will tense up. Just allow the areas of the abdomen and diaphragm to expand around to your back, and the expansion will naturally draw in air through the nose.

Necessary Starting Point

A state of relaxation or stillness within is a necessary starting point for any healing work or contemplative journey. If I am not relaxed and in a state of inner wholeness, then I may transfer frequencies of anxiety and tenseness, along with the level of consciousness I am currently holding to my client.

People trust you when they come for help. If I am feeling out of balance within, then I will see them as broken and needing fixing, and any beliefs they hold about not deserving healing will be solidified. If I am centered in a consciousness of wholeness, that frequency will be in the room and surround that person when they enter the healing space. Who and what I am in that moment is what I will radiate to that person and also what I will imprint on to the energy matrix of the healing space.

Placing Your Focus

In using sound, the focus on consciousness will affect the quality of sound. The difference between a master musician and a technically proficient player is consciousness. That is what makes us shiver when we hear someone sing or play an instrument—the consciousness of the musician talking to us. The same goes for healing. The consciousness of the facilitator will affect the quality of the sound, both sung and unsung, played and unplayed, that is used in a healing practice.

Something to Ponder: Consciousness is the unseen part of the orchestra that your body and voice co-create with when you seek to use sound in healing. Sound body, sound mind, sound consciousness ... and that is where you begin.

Singing the Flames of Source

Many of the frequencies now coming into the earth oscillate at a very high frequency. When seen with the inner eye, they appear as flames. They are *flames of consciousness*, and you can co-create with them to transmute modified, limited, misdirected, and misaligned energies into Divine Source energy (sparkling pearlescent white light).

Use the flames daily to help yourself painlessly release outmoded ways of thinking and acting and accelerate your spiritual growth. You can also co-create with the flames to help you or your client release emotional baggage.

> By the Power of my own Divine Self, I now send all the energies in my biofields that are not mine back to their owner or point of origin, in all time-space continua, all the way back to Source.

Alternatively, you could say,

> By the Power of my own Divine Self, I now transmute all misqualified, misdirected, and misaligned energies in my biofields into Divine Source energies, in all time-space continua, all the way back to Source.

Or you could say,

> By the Power of my own Divine Self, I now send all the energies in my biofields that are not mine, in all time-space

continua, parallel worlds, and alternate realities, back to Source for their next highest level of evolution.

The statements above don't have to be exact. Just make sure it's by the power of your own Divine Self. Otherwise, use whatever words feel right to you and command that it be so. You can also add words concerning tearing up or voiding any contracts or vows that brought or kept those energies in your biofields. Once you command it, then take a moment and feel the release, the sense of freedom in your energetic fields. That will make it more real for you.

Client Preparation

Speak the following to the client:

1. (Client's name), put your attention on the space in the center of your chest about an inch below where your neck bones come together. This is a place where a tiny Rainbow Flame of Divine Source is located. Imagine this Rainbow Flame and place a little you in that flame.
2. Now put a comfortable chair in the light. Seat yourself in the chair and let the flame shine around and through every cell of your body. Gently inhale the energy of the flame, and on the exhale, expand the flame so it flows down and connects to your earth star chakra in the earth's core. Breathe and expand the flame so it flows up through your crown chakra to connect to a point of frequency you name as the Divine Source.
3. Finally, breathe and expand the Rainbow Flame through the pores of your skin.

4. Breathe and expand the flame so it becomes a Rainbow Flame pillar connecting you to the Divine Source and to your own harmonic known as your earth star within the earth. This flame is the consciousness of the Divine Presence, the Rainbow Flame of wholeness and perfection.

5. Take some time, relax, and let yourself melt into and as the Rainbow Flame.

6. (Client's name), continue to be aware of yourself as the Rainbow Flame pillar. Now send a mini you into the center of the pillar. As the mini you, turn around, and see/imagine a doorway. Go through that doorway, and when you do, you will see a hill with a building upon it. Let yourself go to that building by just thinking about it.

7. When you arrive at the building, look around. Are trees and flowers there? What kind of building is it? Does it need repair? Take a moment and make changes if you wish. This is your inner temple, so you can create it to be whatever you want. Remember, energy follows thought, so you just have to think of the changes you wish to make, and it happens.

8. Now climb the steps and go up to the door. Take a look at the door. There might (or might not) be a message on the door for you. If there is, take a moment to embody the message. If one is not there, that is all right too. (Pause.) When you are ready, open the door and walk in.

9. Take a look around and see what your temple looks like. Make changes to reflect what you feel your temple should look like. (Pause.)

10. Go further into the temple now, and you will notice an altar at the far end with an Eternal Flame burning on it. Placed near the altar is a comfortable chair, your chair—a place of rest. Sit down on that chair and just relax. As you relax,

a stream of light comes down from above you, enters your crown, and fills every part of your body. It then continues on down through the earth, where it wraps around the core and anchors you. Let yourself breathe in that light for a few moments. (Pause.)

11. In front of you now appears a Crystal Rainbow Flame, the Freedom Flame. As you notice the flame, it spreads, encircling you in a ring of transforming love.

12. The Rainbow Flame can assist you in releasing that which no longer serves you. It is time now to release the life-denying energies that no longer serve you.

13. Imagine the hands of your mini self now reach out and take hold of any energy that appears dense, chaotic, dark, and so on. In your mind, you can name it. For example, throw resentment into the flame. See it explode into sparkling white light. Now toss envy and shame. Next comes pain and anger. As they touch the flame, they are transmuted into original Divine Source energies. And the flame grows higher and gets brighter and brighter. Throw hate into the flame … and now beliefs and concepts of sin. See or imagine the explosion of distortions into light and love all around you.

14. Now throw regret into the flame. You did the best you could at that point in time. Transmute all your regrets into Source energy. Let all your "what ifs" be transmuted by the flame now.

15. Allow the flame to expand as it grows higher and brighter. As you release into the flame, the flame in your chest starts to glow and spread throughout your body.

16. Continue to peel the onion-skin layers of whatever energies no longer serve you. There is no need to name them. Just

throw them into the flame and feel your heart space becoming warmer.

17. The Rainbow Flame in the center of your chest, your Eternal Flame spark, reaches out to the flame around you, and all the flames become one flame. The lights become one light. You become the center of the flame, and the light continues to expand around you. Above your head, sparkles of silver and gold stream through and around your bodies, and as the frequencies come into your biofields, allow your mouth to open and start toning.

18. Allow yourself to feel the flames. They are Flames of Consciousness, and as you connect with that consciousness, that consciousness will expand out on the sound. Imagine combining the flames and the sound. Send the sound to all areas that feel discordant, chaotic, sluggish, or dense. Intend wholeness.

19. When it feels complete, just rest in the frequency. Allow yourself time to come back into yourself. Feel your hands in your hands; feel your feet in your feet. Breathe consciously several breaths and then open your eyes.

Helping the Earth

Singing down the Flames of Divine Source can help stabilize the energetic grids on the earth. They can also help you build accelerator seats, places of higher energy that help accelerate your spiritual energy process. They are wonderful for meditation.

1. Put your attention on the space in the center of your chest about an inch below where your neck bones come together. This is a place where a tiny Rainbow Flame of Divine

Source is located. Imagine this Rainbow Flame and place a little you in that flame.

2. Now either stand or put a comfortable chair in the light. Seat yourself in the chair and let the flame shine around and through every cell of your body. Gently inhale the energy of the flame, and on the exhale, expand the flame so it flows down and connects to your earth star chakra in the earth's core.

3. Gently inhale the energy of the flame, and on the exhale, expand the flame so it flows up to Source.

4. Finally breathe and expand the flame through the pores of your skin.

5. Breathe and expand the flame so it becomes a Rainbow Flame pillar connecting you to Source and to your own harmonic known as your earth star within the earth. This flame is the consciousness of the Divine Presence, the flame of wholeness and perfection.

6. Take some time, relax, and let yourself melt into and as the flame. Continue to be aware of yourself as the Rainbow Flame pillar.

7. Imagine as you inhale that the energy of the Rainbow Flame pillar is flowing into you. As you exhale, the breath expands both you and the pillar. Breathe as the pillar on both the inhale and the exhale, knowing yourself as the pillar.

8. Open your mouth and start toning as the pillar. Allow the flames to come down through you and out on the sound as you tone. Focus on be-ing the consciousness of Source.

9. Imagine yourself as a Rainbow Flame sound pillar, radiating the sound tones of Source perfection into the ground under your feet, connecting with other Source energies, as they

flow and build a sound-light pattern of Source energy through the earth.

10. When it feels complete, just rest in the frequency. Allow yourself time to come back into yourself. Feel your hands in your hands; feel your feet in your feet. Breathe consciously several breaths. Then open your eyes.

Intent

Aligning with Source means your focus is on wholeness, on Oneness, on Divine Right Order. As you sing or tone, the consciousness of Divine Right Order will radiate out to others through you. This is where intent comes in. If your intent is for your own healing, then that is where the energies will be directed.

Your intent, propelled by your thoughts, becomes your operational instructions and will lay the energetic template to be filled out by the frequencies flowing through and as you.

If your intent is to facilitate healing for someone else, then when you tone, the sound will help your client align with Divine Right Order to start their own healing process.

> **Something to Ponder:** Because sound or vibration is what starts the creation process, "In the Beginning was the Word," then sound can be used to transmute chaotic energies. It can also be used to fill out templates and begin manifestation of healing on all levels: physical, mental, emotional, and spiritual. In this way, the totality of a person is allowed to come into balance, spiritual evolution accelerates, and the connection with higher aspects of self becomes stronger.

Developing a Toning Session

I stumbled upon how to use my voice to scan the body over twenty years ago. I noticed that often when I started vocalizing, I would feel a heavy drag on the sound coming from my voice. It would feel rusty, continue to go flat, or feel like it took so much effort to get the sound to go up into the resonating chambers in the head. Then after a few minutes of warming up, I would sense/feel little pops in my head, and suddenly my voice would start sounding clear and resonant.

One day it came to me that there was heavy energy around my head, or perhaps the energy was blocked in that area, and that is why it would feel heavy or the sound would keep going flat no matter what I did. Furthermore, when I would sense/feel those pops in my head, I realized it meant the heavy energy or energy blockage was breaking up. This "aha" moment was the beginning of a lifetime journey into sound healing.

There are many ways to use sound in a healing practice. You can use the voice, crystal bowls, tuning forks, Tibetan bowls, drums, rattles, chimes, or any of the orchestral instruments. Yet you may find, as I did, that as you grow spiritually within your journey into sound healing, your voice becomes the crystal bowl, the tuning fork, or all the instruments.

Using Vowel Sounds

Vowels are integral to toning. They open a space within you that allows creation to take place. Within this creative space, you and the vowels can dance and play, shaping sound with how large or small the space is within your mouth, head, and even body. You can add tonal effects using different parts of your mouth, throat, and tongue, which all serve to make the sound dance in different ways, allowing the sound waves to change their pattern and shape. Since people are all different and respond to sound in multiple ways, a variety of sound patterns and shapes could affect healing of a wider range of people.

When I started learning to tone, I started by using different vowel sounds and played with singing or toning the sounds toward the inside of my face. Since this was where I was attempting to focus my voice, it seemed the obvious place to start. I tried all five vowel sounds but found that using an "eee" vowel sound seemed to give me the fastest effect. After a bit of toning, I started sensing/feeling pops in my face or within my sinuses. And after several of these pops, my voice would clear.

This use of toning gave me the thought to try it on other areas of my body. I would start toning and mentally send it over various areas of my body, starting with areas I was having issues with. Often I used my hand to point toward the area I was directing the sound to, just to reinforce the idea that the sound was being focused toward a certain area and not to the whole room. I would find that when I directed the sound toward an area that hurt, such as my knee, then the tone would go flat or sound dull. Sometimes it felt like I was pushing against a heavy weight with the sound.

Developing a Sequence

I next learned to develop a sequence. I would make a sound. And then following the flow of energy into the body, I would start at the top of my head and go down the trunk of the body, then down each leg, and finally down each arm. I would mentally make a note of where the sound went flat or dull. I would do this scan several times, making note of where the blockages were in relation to the major chakras, the energy centers of the body. Location of these blockages gave me an idea where and how I was blocking the energies: was it the physical, my thoughts, my emotions, or my relationship to Source?

Directing the Sound

I would then start toning a vowel sound, directing it in areas around the blockage. I would work my way in toward the perceived blockages, and when I got to the spots where the sound and pitch of my voice went flat or dull, I would try different vowel sounds, trying to break through the blockages. I found that the Ē sound (like in bee) cut through heavy energy very quickly, the ooh sound (like in coo) was soothing, and the aah sound (like in ma) was grounding. I continued to work sonically with the blockage until suddenly the energy resistance I felt left, and my voice magically went back on key and was resonant once more. I would then sooth the area with an ooh sound. Then I would go on to the next area of blockage.

> **Something to Ponder:** Scanning and directing sound this way can work with any modality or energetic structure. It will work with any system, whether it utilizes chakras, axiatonal lines, hara lines, or a healing energy system such as Kathara or Reiki. Sound is the basic structure of creation and will work with the intent and consciousness of the practitioner.

Etheric Sound Surgery

Sound assists greatly in etheric surgery. In etheric sound surgery, we use vocally produced sound or toning to weaken or cut through the links of foreign energetic structures within the etheric energy body so they can be easily lifted out or transmuted. We also use toning to weave energetic structures together, build or rebuild energy grids, and sonically cut through channels of blocked energy.

Many energetic blockages appear to the inner eye as third-dimensional symbols. For example, if people are having difficulty feeling energy in their hands or feet, I may get a thought picture in my mind of a pair of handcuffs, manacles, or rope tied around the client's wrists or feet. If they frequently clear their throat or dislike wearing anything around their necks, I might see a noose around their neck. These are all symbolic pictures of blockages whose origins may originate either in their current lifetime or perhaps in other simultaneous lifetimes (what we call past lives). They will come up in layers to be released.

These pictures are often caused by trauma, and the emotional and mental state of the person during that current or simultaneous lifetime event will imprint the structures within the energetic bodies. The imprint will remain in the energetic bodies there long after the third-dimensional structure is removed and will result in an energetic blockage.

Invasive procedures such as physical or dental surgery can cause holes to appear in the auric field. If they are not repaired, the result could be energy leakage.

Finally, those people on a conscious spiritual path often need assistance in building energetic templates or repairing energetic grids. Toning can help repair and build new template structures to help stabilize energy and strengthen energy holding and running capacity.

Basic Etheric Surgery

1. Close your eyes and take several deep breaths to relax and center yourself. Slow the breath, making sure you breathe from your abdomen. As you expand your abdomen, allow the breath to also expand your diaphragm and lungs in conjunction with it. Breathe in and allow the breath to flow to all areas of your body, and as you exhale, breathe out all the tension you have accumulated. Inhale … hold … breathe out as you mentally say "I am relaxed. I am peace. I am Divine Source now. I am One with All There Is now."
2. Build your pillar of sound-light. You can do this either mentally or with actual sound, toning as you imagine a pillar of sound-light reaching up to Source and down to the center of the earth where you connect via your earth star chakra. Ask the client's higher aspects of self to assist.
3. Start toning a vowel sound, directing it in areas around the blockage. Work your way in sonically toward the perceived blockages. When you get to the spots where the sound and pitch of your voice went flat or dull, tone different vowel sounds to try to break through the blockages. If the blockage feels heavy, use an Ē sound (like in bee) to cut through heavy energy very quickly.
4. If it feels like it may be more than just stuck energy, let your brain relax and ask your higher self to show you the issue. Allow the pictures you need to see flow into your head.

The pictures may be symbolic or as a result of energetic trauma, so you may see nets, manacles, ropes, mesh, and so on. Allow these pictures or mental impressions to act as a map for your toning.

5. Use your hand or fingers to point to an area, and with the map in your mind, tone toward the areas where the blockage appears to be attached. An Ē sound, what I call a nasty Ē sound, works well here. This type of Ē is one that feels like you're toning it with a sneer on your face because your teeth are showing and you are directing the sound from your teeth up toward the back of your nose and out the front of your face. Use this sound to disconnect the energetic structure from the energy bodies. Then use your hand to sweep the disconnected energy up and out of the field toward a flame, or imagine a flame surrounding the energy and transforming it into sparkling white light. Soothe the areas of the energy where the structure was attached with whatever color wants to come co-create with you. You will often see a golden-silver pink appear in your mind. If not, that is all right. Just ask the client's Higher Self what colors are needed and allow whatever you receive to flow.

6. If there appears to be a hole in the aura, use your creative imagination to facilitate the closing of it. Imagination is how you give operational instructions when you co-create with Source frequency. You can close auric holes in several different ways. One way is to sing an ooh (like in coo), which is very soothing. While toning this ooh, use your hands to brush the energy fields, imagining you're moving the energy to loosen it and fill it in. Another way is to imagine you are sewing it shut with golden-silver–colored

thread that is directed on the sound. You can also use sound to fill the hole with a golden-silver mesh, using more of the sound to smooth and soothe the edges. When something is removed, a void is created, and the issue can re-create itself. Filling a hole or void with Source energy prevents this.

7. If an area needs to be stabilized or the entire field anchored, use an aah sound (like in ma).

8. Once stabilized, go on to the next area of blockage.

9. Continue on to part 4 of "Standing in the Presence," which follows in the next chapter, if you are using etheric surgery as part of a total session. Otherwise, when finished, use your hands to brush the energy field from the top of the head down to the feet. Then smooth the energy field using gentle circular motions.

10. Release the client into the hands of Source, using whatever form you like. Allow this high energy to surround and penetrate the client for protection and accelerated healing and growth.

11. The last step consists of gratitude, often simply saying, "Thank you, Source!" Allow yourself to remain in a feeling state of thankfulness, appreciation, and gratitude.

12. To help the client embody the healing, assist them in developing statements, invocations, affirmative prayers, or spiritual mind treatments they can use in the weeks following the session.

Something to Ponder: How else can you use creative imagination to facilitate healing of either your client or yourself?

Standing in the Presence

Facilitating the Sound Healing Session

Trust is a very important aspect of healing. When people decide to receive healing treatments, they put themselves in a vulnerable position. The act of opening oneself to healing also opens oneself to mental and energetic imprinting. This means the facilitator must be centered and focused on wholeness both before and during the healing treatment. If the facilitator tends to let the mind stray during treatment, there is a real possibility that the facilitator will take on the client's stuff and then imprint whatever they are thinking onto the client. If at any time the facilitator's mind wanders, then they must step back and get recentered before engaging once again in co-creating healing with the client. Being centered ensures the client will only receive thoughts of wholeness.

Co-creating healing is a sacred process. Your responsibility as a facilitator is to go into your own sacred inner space and bring the client into that space also. I once had a teacher who said, "When we practice the healing arts, we should bring the other person into our meditation with us." Meditation is the act of coming into alignment with a Divine Presence, by whatever name we know this Presence. Alignment with the Presence is alignment with love, with purity, with wholeness. Alignment with a state of wholeness allows the client the opportunity to come into wholeness on all levels. The following is the process I use to know the Oneness and connection with perfect wholeness with my client. Feel free to modify it for your own use.

Client Preparation

Speak the following to the client:

1. (Client's name), put your attention on the space in the center of your chest about an inch below where your neck bones come together. This is a place where a tiny Rainbow Flame of Divine Source is located. Imagine this Rainbow Flame and place a little you in that flame.

2. Now put a comfortable chair in the light. Seat yourself in the chair and let the flame shine around and through every cell of your body. Gently inhale the energy of the flame, and on the exhale, expand the flame so it flows down and connects to your earth star chakra in the earth's core. Breathe and expand the flame so it flows up to Source.

3. Finally breathe and expand the flame through the pores of your skin.

4. Breathe and expand the flame so it becomes a Rainbow Flame pillar connecting you to the Divine Source and to your own harmonic known as your earth star within the earth. This flame is the consciousness of the Divine Presence, the flame of wholeness and perfection.

5. Take some time, relax, and let yourself melt into and as the flame.

> **Note:** Spoken *I Am* statements aligned with Source energies are a powerful invocational healing modality. It has been my experience that the spoken *I Am* work facilitates and accelerates changes. Speaking the *I Am* part out loud is very effective as it allows the words to imprint and resonate in the client's energy fields.

Mentally or verbally speak the following six steps.

Step One: Recognition

1. There is only one Creator, one Divine Source, one Universal Substance, one Mind.
2. Out of this One, (client's name) and I were created.

Step Two: Alignment

1. Since we were created from the same substance, (client's name) and I are connected and reflect the divinity from which we were created. We are One with the Divine Source, with the Creator, with universal substance. Since the divinity from which we were created is perfect, the very core of our being, our spiritual blueprint, is perfect and whole.
2. I now call on Source to use me as an instrument of healing grace for (client's name)'s highest good and the highest good of all creation.

Step Three: Letting Source Flow

The facilitator now starts the energy-healing facilitation process, using intuition as a guide for whatever needs to be done. In this process, we cover scanning, directing sound, and using other modalities.

Since energy comes into our energy biofields via the chakras above our heads, through our pineal and then down through the rest of the body, it is recommended that hand placement and toning start from the top of the body to the feet. There is no right or wrong order for where to start the facilitation specifically. It just depends where your inner voice leads you.

Scanning and Directing Sound with the Voice

1. Choose a vowel sound. Following the flow of energy into the body, start toning at the top of the head and go down the trunk of the body, down each leg, and then down each arm. Mentally make a note of where the sound went flat or dull.
2. Do this scan several times, making note where the blockages were in relation to the chakras, the energy centers of the body. Location of blockages will give you an idea on what level energies are being blocked: physical, mental thoughts, emotions, or perhaps the client's relationship to Source.
3. Direct the sound into the area around the blockages. Work your way in toward the perceived blockages, and when you get to the spots where the sound and pitch of your voice went flat or dull, try to break through the blockages using different vowel sounds. Do not be afraid to experiment.
4. Some blockages will respond to one sound, or it could take several different sounds to move a blockage. Try the Ē sound (like in bee) to cut through heavy energy very quickly, the ooh sound (like in coo) to soothe and fill in holes, and the aah sound (like in ma) for grounding the physical and for anchoring energetic grids and templates.
5. Continue to work sonically with the blockage until suddenly the energy resistance leaves and your voice goes back on key and sounds resonant once more. Soothe the area with an ooh sound. Then go on to the next area of blockage.
6. Option: Sometimes when I tone, I think, "Let there be light!" This sometimes has interesting effects as this statement is one of the original divine creation statements.

Bowls and Percussion Instruments

1. When you finish toning, take a few deep breaths and relax.
2. Use your healing bowls and percussion instruments to help with the healing process at this stage. Examples of percussion instruments used include gongs, rattles, drums, and chimes. Along with Divine Source energy and the assistance of the client's and your own higher aspects of self, you can also include at this stage other modalities such as aromatherapy, color healing, and etheric surgery.

Step Four: Stating Truth

Invocational Healing

Near the end of the treatment, go to the client's head, put your hands on either side of the head, and state the following (or something similar):

1. (Client's name), continue to put your attention on your Rainbow Flame pillar. Sense, feel, or see that flame pillar, and continue to breathe as the pillar. Continue to let the flame shine through and all around you.
2. I stand here as my own Rainbow Flame pillar, and I now join you in the Presence of Source. As I stand there with you, we recognize that we are one in consciousness, for we are connected through the Flame of Source. Because this Divine Source Presence is also the I Am Presence, I will state and recognize the truth of your being using *I Am* statements. Let the sound and the feeling of the words

resonate throughout your total self. Feel free to repeat them after me, either mentally or out loud.

The following are examples of ones I have used. Feel free to make up others as your intuition leads you.

a. I open myself to the healing of Source, I Am, for I Am perfect healing.
b. I open myself to the wholeness of Source, I Am, for I Am perfect wholeness.
c. I open myself to the love of the Source, I Am, for I Am perfect love.
d. I open myself to my I Am Presence, for I Am This I Am.
e. I open myself to the (peace, wisdom, abundance, etc.) of Source, I Am, for I Am perfect (peace, wisdom, abundance, etc.) now!
f. I Am Divine Right Order, and Divine Right Order flows through my body and my life continuously.

Note: The words "I open" cause the energy fields to open receptively and allow the statements of truth to penetrate. I Am is the name of Source. When you say "I Am," you take on the mantle of Source authority and create whatever you state following those words. Therefore, stating "I Am peace" creates peace in your life and facilitates peace in the life of the person you are stating it for. That is why it is so important to be aware of your thoughts and words. Throwaway phrases such as "I am sorry … I am sick … I am tired" creates exactly that. You will end up tired, sick, and full of sorrow. So be aware and start consciously creating a life-affirming future for yourself now.

Step Five: Letting Go

1. Upon completing the "I Am" work (step four), release the client into the hands of Source, using whatever form you like. Some practitioners imagine themselves putting the client into a pair of giant hands, naming those hands as Source's hands. Others release verbally (e.g., and so it is, blessed be, amen, etc.), or do a combination of the two. Whatever way works best for you is perfect.
2. Smooth out the aura and then state mentally or verbally something similar to, "Source, I now put (client's name) into your hands, knowing that all is well and in Divine Order. So be it, and so I let it be so. And so it is."
3. Allow this high energy to surround and penetrate the client for protection and accelerated healing and growth.

Step Six: Gratitude

The last step consists simply of "Thank You _____!" (fill in the blank)

How you show gratitude is up to you. It could consist of just remaining in a feeling state of thankfulness, a verbal thank-you at the end of the step four verbal release, or even singing or chanting. The main focus though should be in feeling thankful for the opportunity to radiate the Divine Source and hold the doorway of consciousness open that all may enter.

Whatever comes to you to do is what is perfect for that client and you at that moment in time. The process of performing a healing treatment is an intuitive process. Intuition is the voice of the Divine Source. So listen. And by listening, healing becomes a prayer.

Something to Ponder: What do you do before, during, and after a session to help a client feel safe?

Something to Ponder: What can you do to become more intuitive? Do you practice listening to others and to yourself? Do you trust yourself?

Something to Ponder: If you do not trust yourself, what inner healing work do you need to do? Trusting yourself is the first step toward building trust between you and the client. If you trust yourself, they will trust you, based on the energy you are radiating.

Expanding Awareness of
You as Divine Source

We all are sparks of Divine Source. As we clear our energetic body and align with the Divine Source, our sparks merge with the fire of our personal twelfth-dimensional self. As we expand further to the core of our self, this fire merges with and becomes the Flame of Divine Source. The Flame of Divine Source is pure pearlescent white, yet it holds all of the colors of creation within it.

The purpose of these meditations is to start the sparking within the flames and thereby open inner portals/gates in each of the density levels to allow us to expand vertically through different inner frequency bands to the Divine Source. (Three-dimensional frequency bands equal one density level; therefore dimensions one, two, and three equate to one density level.)

As each level merges, the individual flames take on the appearance of a spherical sun sparking, the sparks of living consciousness flying out into the void that exists between density levels. As we consciously breathe in Divine Source energy, energetic locks open up to allow access into and through the void. Our conscious thought of alignment with Divine Source becomes like a pebble thrown into a pool, with our conscious sense of self a pool, rippling out in ever-expanding waves of frequency sparks. Flames expand through the void to merge with the next sun, through which the activation of personal consciousness expands and fuels the fire and flames of Divine Source at each dimensional and density level.

As our consciousness moves closer to the Divine Source,

we sense the winds of Source fan the flames, creating sparks of the living consciousness, which serve as a beacon home. The Divine Source is not stationary or without movement. The winds of Divine Source energy eternally send forth sparks to allow for creation of the flames of living consciousness.

It is very important to be centered in and as the Divine Source when acting as a conduit for healing energies. The challenge is to be centered constantly, to take the temple with you wherever you go—whatever you do. This centering anchors the Divine Source energies and sanctifies the very ground on which you walk.

The following exercises give you a way to come into contact with your higher power, protecting and expanding your own frequencies of sound and light. With daily practice, you will soon develop a feeling of abundance, safety, and knowingness as well as a greater feeling connection to the Divine Source.

Tower of Power Meditation

1. Close your eyes and put your attention on the space in the center of your chest about an inch below where your neck bones come together. This is a place where a tiny Rainbow Flame of Divine Source is located. Imagine this Rainbow Flame and place a little you in that flame.
2. Now relax within the light. You can sit down on a chair if you wish, or you can remain standing, soaking up the light into the very cellular structure of your body.
3. Expand the flame. Make it as broad and as deep as you can. Connect it to the throat and solar plexus areas.
4. Continue to expand the light up to the forehead and down to the lower abdomen.

5. Brighten the light. Make it sparkling and glimmering with rainbow colors, silver and gold. Expand the light out and around your body as you continue to expand it up to the crown and down to the base of your spine.
6. Let the light travel down to your knees and on down to the soles of your feet.
7. Now expand the light up to a spot about a foot above you head and on down to a foot below your feet.
8. Gently inhale the energy of the flame. On the exhale, expand the flame so it flows down and connects to your earth star chakra in the earth's core. Breathe and expand the flame so it flows up to the Divine Source. Once connected, ensure the light is as clear, sparkling, and bright as you can.

These steps open your inner rainbow arc pillar of light connection to Source and would look like a bright sparkling tube or pillar of energy with all the colors of the rainbow, silver and gold, running through a bright, sparkling pearlescent white. It would run from the earth core all the way up through the center of your body and out into deep space. The bottom of your pillar is anchored within your earth star chakra at earth core to allow stability of the energy within your physical body.

The Tower of Power can also be used to anchor different frequencies of light into the earth. Daily or weekly, infuse your column of light with a different color of the rainbow. In addition to anchoring the light, you will accelerate the clearing of issues related to the misuse of that frequency of light. Once you have anchored the seven rainbow colors, you can go on to the higher frequencies of light such as peach, aquamarine, emerald green, magenta, gold, silver, opalescent white, and rainbowed crystal clear light.

Expanding Awareness of You as Divine Source Meditation

1. Activate your pillar connection to Divine Source via whatever method you are comfortable with. You can use the technique above, or you can just imagine a sphere of pure golden and pearlescent white light at the earth's core and inhale this sphere of golden-white light all the way upward, through the center of your body and out the top of your head, out into deep space.

2. Close your eyes and take several deep, gentle breaths. Inhale peace and calm. Then exhale peace and calm through your body. (Simply think peace and calm as you inhale and exhale as if that is what each breath is.) Allow each part of your body to relax. Mentally tell your brain it can relax also.

3. Imagine a golden and pearlescent white spark of conscious light in the center of your high chest, just below the point where your collarbones come together. This is where your Eternal Spark is located.

4. This Eternal Spark is a spark of your conscious identity, a small mini you, sparkling and radiating the brightest light you can imagine. This is the point of your physical body that connects to all of your identities throughout the time matrix and to the Divine Source.

5. Picture your inner pillar and inhale frequency from the pillar into your Eternal Spark. Then exhale the sparkling light gently upward within your vertical pillar.

6. Take three more inhale and exhale breaths, and on each exhale breath, see your small mini self traveling upward through your pillar. You will notice a pearlescent white light coming into view at the top of your vertical pillar.

The distance from your physical body does not matter. Simply allow your small mini self to travel upward and notice the bright pearlescent light coming into your view. The bright pearlescent light is the pure consciousness field of the Divine Source.

7. Allow your mini self to step into this field of Source, pure, bright pearlescent white light energy. Become aware of the feelings you will feel from within this expanded space of Source. Feel the love and joy of Source all around and within your mini self. Feel the love of Source gently brush the cheek of your mini self. You may even become aware of the consciousness of the Divine Source smiling at you.

8. Using a gentle breathing rhythm, inhale into the Eternal Spark of your mini self, and imagine as you inhale, that the body of your mini self is being filled with the pure light of Source energy. As you feel your mini self become completely filled with Source energy, notice that your vertical pillar becomes saturated with the bright, pearlescent white light of Source energy.

9. You may notice and feel as if you become one with the bright pearlescent light that previously seemed to be a space you entered into. You are now emerged completely within the pure consciousness of Source.

10. Continue the gentle breathing rhythm of inhaling more of the bright pearlescent white light of Source into your mini self and into your vertical pillar. From the awareness of your mini self, become aware of your physical 3D body as if you can see it positioned way below the location of your mini self and become aware that your vertical pillar is also filling your physical 3D body with the pure loving joy of Source that is much stronger within the pearlescent white light.

11. On the next inhale breath, inhale as if you are inhaling your mini self back down through your vertical pillar and back into the location of your physical 3D body and into the Eternal Spark of the physical 3D body. Exhale gently into the Eternal Spark of the 3D physical body as you position your mini self back into your physical body.

12. Take three gentle inhale/exhale breaths from within the Eternal Spark of your physical body, and on each exhale breath, expand the pure pearlescent white light held within your mini self at the Eternal Spark throughout your entire physical body form. As you strengthen and expand the pure light of Divine Source consciousness into your physical body, notice that every molecule and cell of your physical body starts to tingle. Your skin starts to feel as if it is tingling from the inside out.

13. Remember the wonderful feeling of the loving joy of Source that you felt while you were within the pure bright pearlescent white light of the Divine Source. Feel that loving joy fill your entire physical body on each exhale breath you take to expand that energy within your entire physical body.

14. As you continue to expand your mini self within your physical body form, become aware of the point when the mini self has expanded to the size of your physical body. The hands and feet of your mini self merge with the hands and feet of your physical body form. Your entire physical body is now radiating with the pure, bright pearlescent light of Divine Source energy. It is now filled with the loving joy that the Divine Source feels for you eternally.

15. Gently take several more breaths and expand the pure, bright pearlescent white light of Divine Source energy

through the pores of your skin, allowing your glowing form to breathe as the Divine Light of Source.

16. Allow yourself to remain still and quiet as long as you desire to simply be with the loving joy of Divine Source energy. When you are ready, bring your focus back into the area around you and allow yourself to move around.

Something to Ponder: You allow more of the pure energy of the Divine Source to expand and awaken within your physical body each time you consciously connect with the pearlescent white light of the Divine Source, and allow yourself to become conscious of the loving joy of the Divine Source that is a part of every fiber of your being.

Something to Practice: You can very quickly return to the pure expanded space of Divine Source consciousness any time you desire. Simply activate your vertical pillar and send a spark of your consciousness upward through your vertical pillar until you become aware of the pure pearlescent white light of Divine Source energy. Then inhale that spark of your consciousness back into the high center point of your physical body and expand the pure light of the Divine Source within your physical body. Each time you do this process, you will notice the tingling feeling within the physical body becoming stronger. **Note:** This meditation is a simple process for breathing expanded awareness of pure Divine Source energy into the physical body to assist with energetic healing. You can use it to release anything from your personal hologram to allow it to come into alignment with the Divine Source. This is also the space you center yourself within as you facilitate toning and energy healing sessions.

The Dream

I had a dream, and in this vision, I was trying to break through some concrete-like blockages in my body and energy field. I was told to consider using the sound fields and song to open blockages. Sing them open instead of trying to blow them open. I was then handed a crystal with a song in it to sing.

I started singing, and as the energy built the crystal transformed into the song—notes, measures, and all of the symbols of a song but all in crystal and multicolored. Different shapes, colors, and tempo, all of them were singing, moving, and flowing all through the body. I was told that this is what DNA is supposed to be. View the ladder of the DNA sideways and see that it is a symbol of a piece of music, a clef between the outside layers of the DNA with the ladder rungs inside as the notes and staves of music.

As the notes and measures went through my body, the measures were like banners waving and moving, and the notes were constantly changing—flashing on and off, dancing, changing size and tempo, and changing colors. I saw pastels, jewel colors, opalescence, and sparkles, all glittering, dancing, and singing. So it was a combination of light and sounds dancing together and interweaving the healing and wholeness that is needed as it went along. One of the measures took root in my spine, and where each vertebrae or rib came into it, there was a note in place doing its work.

Think of a complete opus of music with all of its parts and variations. It takes time yet is timeless. Sound is a living, breathing consciousness that flows in flexible ways to where it is needed. We sing our song and allow our song and the song of Source to dance a healing pattern toward wholeness and unification of the organism on all levels of consciousness. We are the entire symphony, the melody, the counterpoint, and the harmony. We sing and dance as the consciousness of the Word. In this feeling of wholeness, we become both the singer and the song. In this moment, we are home.

Welcome home to the all within the One.
Welcome home to the place where dreams are spun.
Songs of light sound the rhythm of the poem.
Speak the Word, sound the cadence, welcome home.

Welcome home to the flame of Spirit light.
Welcome home to the land of music bright,
Rainbow magic reveals the perfect tone.
Sing the song, feel the current, welcome home.

Index

R

rainbow flame 56, 57, 58, 59, 60, 72, 75, 80
repairing energetic grids 68
resonating chambers 43, 63
rhythm 2, 37, 38, 39, 40, 83, 88

S

sacred song ix
scan 63, 65, 74
scanning 73
sense/feel xii, 2, 4, 6, 19, 31, 33, 34, 38, 39, 44, 63
sequence 64
singing down the flames 59
slame 60
son/daughter principle 7
soul blueprint 29
soul sounds 19
sound 7
Source ix, 1, 5, 6, 7, 8, 14, 15, 17, 18, 19, 20, 21, 23, 24, 26, 29, 30, 31, 32, 33, 35, 37, 38, 39, 40, 43, 46, 47, 48, 49, 50, 51, 55, 56, 57, 58, 59, 60, 61, 65, 68, 69, 70, 72, 73, 74, 75, 76, 77, 79, 80, 81, 82, 83, 84, 85, 88
speaking your word 13
spirit 88
Spirit 19, 32
spiritual evolution 14, 61
symbols 7, 9, 10, 67, 87

T

template 2, 3, 4, 5, 9, 17, 18, 61, 68
thoughts xi, 1, 2, 7, 9, 10, 21, 25, 26, 27, 61, 65, 71, 74, 76
Tibetan 30, 35, 63
tone ix, 5, 6, 11, 13, 14, 29, 44, 48, 60, 61, 64, 68, 69, 74, 88
toning 4, 6, 7, 11, 31, 38, 43, 51, 59, 60, 63, 64, 65, 67, 68, 69, 73, 74, 75, 85
tower of power 14, 15, 80, 81
transformation 2
transmute 55, 58, 61
true listening xii
trust 71
truth 14, 15, 75, 76

U

unification 50, 88
universal mind 32

V

vibration xi, 1, 9, 25, 29, 45, 61
violation of spiritual integrity 34
vowels 63

W

wholeness 5, 6, 7, 13, 17, 18, 19, 31, 34, 35, 39, 40, 49, 50, 52, 57, 59, 60, 61, 71, 72, 76, 87, 88
wholeness consciousness 35, 40
wind instruments 3

Made in the USA
Coppell, TX
09 January 2021

47813852R00065